COUNTRY COOKING

Consultant Editor:
Valerie Ferguson

Contents

Introduction 4

Homemade Stocks 6

Techniques 8

Country Soups 10

Fish Dishes 20

Poultry, Game & Meat 28

Vegetarian Dishes 46

Country Desserts & Baked Goods 54

Introduction

The character of country cooking does not depend on geography. Whether you live in a city apartment, a suburban house or a rural cottage, you can enjoy the pleasures of wholesome food, plainly cooked, but packed with flavor. The secret of country cooking is the use of the freshest, seasonal produce. There is something special about the first tender vegetables of the summer and the succulent berries of autumn. Spring lamb is almost a cliché, and what could be more sustaining on a cold winter's day than a potpie brimming with chicken and leeks.

Few people these days have the time to grow vegetables and fruit or to catch wild trout, but modern transportation brings fresh produce to even inner-city stores. Look for a reliable supplier of organic produce, and grow herbs in pots on a windowsill.

Whether you want a dish for a family supper or a celebration, you will find just the right recipe in this superb collection. There are dishes for all occasions, from substantial and nourishing soups to mouthwatering desserts and magnificent roasts. Wherever you live, let a breath of country-fresh air blow through your kitchen.

INTRODUCTION

Homemade Stocks

A sauce or stew is only as good as the stock that it is made from. Stock is easy to make: it basically cooks itself after the first few minutes.

Fish Stock

Makes 8 cups

INGREDIENTS
2 pounds heads and bones and trimmings from white fish
1 onion, thinly sliced
1 carrot, thinly sliced
1 leek, thinly sliced
1 lemon, thinly sliced
8 parsley stems
1 bay leaf
1 cup dry white wine
1 teaspoon black peppercorns

1 Put all the ingredients in a saucepan or flameproof casserole and cover with 7½ cups water. Bring to a boil over medium heat, skimming off any surface foam.

2 Simmer gently for 25 minutes, then strain through a muslin-lined sieve. Cool, then chill. Reduce, if you wish, for storage or freezing.

Vegetable Stock

Makes 7½ cups

INGREDIENTS
1 onion, peeled
2 carrots
2 large celery stalks
small amounts of any of the following:
    leeks, celeriac, parsnip, turnip,
    cabbage, cauliflower, mushroom
2 tablespoons vegetable oil
1 bouquet garni
6 black peppercorns

1 Slice the onion and roughly chop the remaining vegetables. Heat the oil and cook the vegetables until soft and lightly browned. Add the remaining ingredients. Cover with 7½ cups water.

2 Bring to a boil, skim, then partially cover and simmer for 1½ hours. Strain and let cool. Store in the refrigerator for up to 3 days.

Homemade Stocks

Beef Stock

Makes 12 cups

INGREDIENTS
8–10 pounds raw or cooked beef or veal bones and meat
2 large unpeeled onions, halved and root end trimmed
2 medium carrots, cut in large pieces
1 large celery stalk, cut in large pieces
2 leeks, cut in large pieces
1 or 2 parsnips, cut in large pieces
2–4 garlic cloves, peeled
1 large bouquet garni
1 tablespoon black peppercorns

1 Place the bones, meat and vegetables in a large roasting pan and brown in the oven at 450°F for 30–40 minutes, turning occasionally.

2 Transfer to a stock pot, add the remaining ingredients and cover with cold water by at least 1 inch. Bring to a boil over medium heat. Skim off the foam with a spoon as soon as it appears, continuing until it stops.

3 Reduce the heat and simmer very gently, uncovered, for 4–5 hours. Skim occasionally and do not boil. Add boiling water if the level falls below the bones and vegetables.

4 Discard the bones and vegetables. Cool and chill the stock, then scrape off the fat. Remove any additional fat by "wiping" with paper towels.

Chicken Stock

Makes 8 cups

INGREDIENTS
4½ pounds raw chicken carcasses, necks or feet, or cooked carcasses
2 large onions, unpeeled, root end trimmed
3 carrots, cut in large pieces
1 celery stalk, cut in large pieces
1 leek, cut in large pieces
2 garlic cloves, unpeeled and lightly smashed
1 sprig fresh parsley
2 bay leaves

1 Proceed as for Beef Stock, starting at step 2, but simmer for 2 hours.

COOK'S TIP: Make stock whenever you roast a piece of meat on the bone or a bird, or save bones and carcasses in the freezer until you have enough for stock. After making stock, reduce it by at least half and freeze in an ice cube tray. Store the cubes in a freezer bag and add to soups and sauces while frozen. Never add salt to the stock, as it will be concentrated during reduction, and season sauces after adding the stock.

Techniques

Chopping Onions
Many dishes use chopped onions as an essential flavoring, and for stir-fried dishes it is important to keep the pieces even.

1 Peel the onion. Cut it in half and set it cut-side down on a board. Make lengthwise vertical cuts along it, cutting almost but not quite through to the root.

2 Make two horizontal cuts from the stalk end towards the root, but not through it. Cut the onion crosswise to form small, even dice.

Chopping Vegetables
For coarsely chopped vegetables, follow the steps without shaving off curved sides. Alternatively, coarsely chop vegetables in a food processor by pulsing, but take care not to turn them into a purée.

1 Peel the vegetable, if instructed. Cut long vegetables across into pieces 3 inches long. Shave off curved sides.

2 Lay the vegetable flat and cut it lengthwise into uniform slices, according to the size needed, guiding the side of the knife with your knuckles. Stack the slices and cut lengthwise into uniform strips. Gather the strips together and cut across the strips into cubes or fine dice.

TECHNIQUES

Blanching & Refreshing

Vegetables are blanched for several reasons: to loosen skins before peeling, to set color and flavor, and to reduce bitterness. They are often blanched as an initial cooking, when more cooking is to be done by stir-frying or a brief reheating in butter or if they are to be used in a salad. After blanching, most foods are "refreshed" to stop them from cooking any more.

1 To blanch: Immerse the food in a large pan of boiling water. Bring the water back to a boil and boil for the time specified, usually 1–2 minutes. Immediately lift the food out of the water or strain.

2 To refresh: Quickly immerse the food in ice water or hold under cold running water. If the recipe specifies, set aside until it has cooled completely. Drain well.

Chopping Herbs

Chop herbs just before you use them: the flavor will then be at its best.

1 Place the leaves on a clean, dry board. Use a large, sharp cook's knife (if you use a blunt knife, you will bruise the herbs rather than slice them) and chop them until they are as coarse or as fine as needed.

2 Alternatively, use a herb chopper, also called a *mezzaluna*, which is a very useful tool for finely chopping herbs or vegetables and consists of a sharp, curved blade with two handles. Use the *mezzaluna* in a see-saw motion for best results.

COUNTRY SOUPS

Celery Soup

Mild celery with a hint of nutmeg—this fresh-tasting and nourishing creamy soup makes a perfect appetizer.

Serves 4

INGREDIENTS
1 small bunch of celery
1 onion, finely chopped
1 small garlic clove, crushed
few parsley sprigs, chopped
2 bay leaves
1 thyme sprig
2½ cups milk
2 tablespoons butter, softened
¼ cup all-purpose flour
pinch of grated nutmeg
1 egg yolk, beaten
salt and freshly ground black pepper
chopped fresh parsley, to garnish
croutons, to serve

1 Break the bunch of celery into stalks and wash thoroughly. Trim the root ends. Chop the stalks and leaves and put them into a large saucepan.

2 Add the onion, garlic, herbs and just enough water to cover. Bring to a boil and simmer, uncovered, over low heat for about 35 minutes.

3 Bring the milk to a boil. Stir the butter and flour together to make a paste and whisk into the hot milk until just thickened. Cook over low heat, stirring occasionally, for about 10 minutes. Pour into the celery mixture and cook for 5 minutes.

4 Remove and discard the bay leaves and thyme. Using a ladle, spoon the soup into a blender or food processor and process for 1 minute, until smooth. Alternatively, rub through a strainer with the back of a spoon. Return to a clean saucepan and season well.

5 Stir in the grated nutmeg and the beaten egg yolk. Bring the soup almost to the boiling point, then serve garnished with chopped fresh parsley and croutons.

COOK'S TIP: To make croutons, cut the crusts off two thick slices of day-old bread and cut the bread into ¼-inch squares. Heat 2 tablespoons vegetable oil or ¼ cup butter in a frying pan and sauté the cubes, tossing and stirring constantly. Drain on paper towels.

COUNTRY SOUPS

Mushroom & Parsley Soup

Thickened with bread, this rich mushroom soup will warm you up on cold autumn days. It makes a terrific hearty lunch.

Serves 8

INGREDIENTS
6 tablespoons unsalted butter
2 pounds field mushrooms, sliced
2 onions, roughly chopped
2½ cups milk
8 slices white bread
¼ cup chopped fresh parsley
1¼ cups heavy cream
salt and freshly ground black pepper
parsley, to garnish

1 Melt the butter and sauté the mushrooms and onions for about 10 minutes, until soft but not colored. Add the milk.

2 Tear the bread into pieces, drop them into the soup and let the bread soak for 15 minutes.

3 Purée the soup and return it to the pan. Add the parsley, cream and seasoning. Re-heat, but do not let the soup boil. Serve with parsley.

Pumpkin Soup

A classic symbol of the harvest, pumpkin makes a beautifully colored soup that would be perfect for an autumn dinner.

Serves 4

INGREDIENTS
¼ cup butter
1 medium onion, finely chopped
1-pound piece of peeled pumpkin,
 cut into 1-inch cubes
3 cups Chicken Stock
 or water
2 cups milk
pinch of grated nutmeg, plus extra,
 for serving
1½ ounces spaghetti, broken
 into small pieces
6 tablespoons freshly grated
 Parmesan cheese
salt and freshly ground black pepper

1 Heat the butter in a pan. Add the onion and cook gently for 8 minutes, until softened. Stir in the pumpkin, and cook for 3 minutes.

2 Add the stock or water and cook for about 15 minutes, until the pumpkin is tender. Remove from heat.

3 Process the soup in a blender or food processor. Return it to the pan. Stir in the milk and nutmeg and season with salt and pepper. Bring the soup back to a boil. Stir in the spaghetti and cook until tender. Stir in the Parmesan. Serve in individual bowls sprinkled with a little nutmeg.

COUNTRY SOUPS

Baby Carrot & Fennel Soup

Sweet tender carrots find their moment of glory in this delicately spiced soup. The fennel provides a distinctive aniseed flavor without overpowering the carrots.

Serves 4

INGREDIENTS
¼ cup butter
1 small bunch of scallions, chopped
5 ounces fennel bulb, chopped
1 celery stalk, chopped
1 pound new carrots, grated
½ teaspoon ground cumin
5 ounces new potatoes, diced
5 cups Chicken or
   Vegetable Stock
¼ cup heavy cream
salt and freshly ground
   black pepper
¼ cup chopped fresh parsley,
   to garnish

COOK'S TIP: For extra convenience, you can freeze the blended soup in portions before adding the heavy cream, seasoning and parsley. When you are ready to serve, defrost thoroughly and reheat the soup gently before adding the remaining ingredients.

1 Melt the butter in a large saucepan and add the scallions, fennel, celery, grated carrots and ground cumin. Cover and cook for 5 minutes, until the vegetables have softened.

2 Add the potatoes and chicken or vegetable stock, and simmer for another 10 minutes, until the vegetables are tender.

COUNTRY SOUPS

3 Blend the mixture in the pan with a hand-held blender. Stir in the heavy cream and season to taste with salt and freshly ground black pepper. Serve in individual bowls and garnish with chopped fresh parsley.

COUNTRY SOUPS

Leek & Thyme Soup

A filling, heartwarming soup that can be blended into a smooth purée or served as it is here, in its original peasant style.

Serves 4

INGREDIENTS
2 pounds leeks
1 pound potatoes
½ cup butter
1 large fresh thyme sprig
1¼ cups milk
salt and freshly ground
  black pepper
fresh thyme, to garnish (optional)
4 tablespoons heavy cream,
  to serve

1 Trim the leeks. If you are using big winter leeks, strip off all the coarser outer leaves, then cut the leeks into thick slices. Wash under cold running water.

2 Cut the potatoes into rough dice, about 1 inch, and dry thoroughly on absorbent paper towels.

3 Melt the butter in a large saucepan and add the leeks and thyme sprig. Cover and cook for 4–5 minutes, until softened. Add the potato pieces and just enough cold water to cover the vegetables. Re-cover and cook over low heat for 30 minutes.

4 Pour in the milk and season to taste, cover and simmer for another 30 minutes. Some potato will break up, making a lumpy soup.

5 Remove the thyme sprig (the leaves will have fallen into the soup) and serve, adding a tablespoon of cream and a garnish of thyme, if using.

COUNTRY SOUPS

Pea & Ham Soup

Once designed to satisfy the appetite after a hard day on the farm, this hearty soup is just as good after a walk in the fresh air.

Serves 4

INGREDIENTS
2½ cups green split peas
4 strips bacon
1 onion, roughly chopped
2 carrots, sliced
1 celery stalk, sliced
10 cups cold water
1 fresh thyme sprig
2 bay leaves
1 large potato, roughly diced
1 ham hock
freshly ground black pepper

3 Add the onion, carrots and celery to the fat in the pan and cook for 3–4 minutes, until the onion is softened, but not brown. Return the bacon to the pan with the water.

1 Put the peas into a bowl, add just enough cold water to cover and set aside to soak overnight.

4 Drain the peas and add to the pan with the herbs, potato and ham hock. Bring to a boil, reduce the heat, cover and cook gently for 1 hour.

2 Cut the bacon into small pieces. In a large saucepan, dry-fry the bacon for 4–5 minutes or until crisp. Remove from the pan with a slotted spoon.

VARIATION: Yellow split peas can be used instead of green, or try using a mixture of both.

5 Remove the thyme, bay leaves and hock. Process the soup in a blender or food processor until smooth. Return to a clean pan. Cut the meat from the hock and add to the soup. Season with black pepper and serve.

FISH DISHES

Cod with Parsley Sauce

A simple, traditional dish that combines the delicate flavor of cod with a smooth herb-infused sauce.

Serves 4

INGREDIENTS
2 tablespoons butter, plus extra
  for greasing
4 cod fillets or steaks,
  about 8 ounces each
1 bay leaf
6 peppercorns
small bunch of parsley
1 shallot, quartered
¼ cup all-purpose flour
1¼ cups milk
salt and freshly ground
  black pepper
cabbage, to serve (optional)

1 Grease a large flameproof casserole with a little butter. Lay the cod fillets in the pan, skin-side down. Add the bay leaf, peppercorns, parsley stalks and the quartered shallot.

COOK'S TIP: For a stronger parsley flavor, try using the flat-leaf variety for this dish. If that is not available, however, the more familiar curly-leaved variety also makes an excellent sauce.

2 Pour in enough cold water to cover the fish. Bring to a boil and immediately reduce to a gentle simmer. Cook for 5 minutes. Meanwhile, finely chop the parsley tops and set aside.

3 Melt the butter in a saucepan, then stir in the flour and cook gently for 1 minute. Strain the stock from the fish and reserve ⅔ cup. Remove the fish from the pan and keep warm.

4 Gradually add the reserved stock to the flour mixture and continue stirring over medium heat until the sauce is smooth and has thickened.

5 Gradually add the milk and bring to a boil. Reduce the heat and cook the sauce, stirring occasionally, for about 10 minutes. Stir in the chopped parsley and season well. Serve with the fish and cabbage, if desired.

FISH DISHES

Mackerel with Roasted Blueberries

Fresh blueberries burst with flavor when roasted, and their sharpness complements the rich flesh of mackerel very well.

Serves 4

INGREDIENTS
2 tablespoons all-purpose flour
4 small cooked, smoked mackerel fillets
¼ cup unsalted butter
juice of ½ lemon
salt and freshly ground black pepper
lettuce, orange segments and zest, to serve

FOR THE ROASTED BLUEBERRIES
1 pound blueberries
2 tablespoons sugar
1 tablespoon unsalted butter
salt and freshly ground black pepper

1 Preheat the oven to 400°F. Season the flour. Dip each fish fillet into the flour to coat it well.

2 Dice the butter, dot it on the fish fillets and bake for 20 minutes.

3 Place the blueberries, sugar, butter and seasoning in a separate small roasting pan and roast them, basting them occasionally, for 15 minutes. Drizzle the lemon juice on the mackerel and serve with the roasted blueberries, lettuce and orange.

Pan-fried Trout with Bacon

If you can find it, use wild brown trout for its superb flavor, which is vastly superior to that of farmed rainbow trout.

Serves 4

INGREDIENTS
4 trout, cleaned and gutted
¼ cup all-purpose flour
3 ounces bacon
¼ cup butter
1 tablespoon olive oil
juice of ½ lemon
salt and freshly ground
   black pepper
fresh thyme, to garnish
broiled tomatoes, to serve

1 Pat the trout dry with absorbent paper towels and combine the flour and salt and pepper.

2 Roll the trout in the seasoned flour mixture and wrap them tightly in the bacon, excluding the heads.

3 Fry the trout in the butter and oil for 5 minutes on each side. Drizzle with lemon juice and serve with the tomatoes and garnished with thyme.

FISH DISHES

Cod & Spinach Parcels

The best way to serve this dish is to slice each parcel into about four pieces and reveal the large meaty flakes of white fish.

Serves 4

INGREDIENTS
4 6-ounce pieces of thick
    cod fillet, skinned
8 ounces large spinach leaves
½ teaspoon freshly grated nutmeg
3 tablespoons white wine
salt and freshly ground black pepper
lemon wedges and chopped fresh parsley,
    to garnish

2 Blanch the spinach leaves in boiling water for a minute and refresh under cold water.

3 Pat the spinach leaves thoroughly on plenty of absorbent paper towels.

1 Preheat the oven to 350°F. Season the fish well with salt and freshly ground black pepper.

COOK'S TIP: For best results, cover the roasting pan with a loose-fitting lid or a sheet of aluminum foil before poaching in the oven.

4 Wrap the spinach around each fish fillet. Sprinkle with nutmeg. Place in a roasting pan, pour in the wine and poach for 15 minutes. Slice and serve hot with the cooking juices drizzled on the top, garnished with the lemon wedges and parsley.

FISH DISHES

Creamy Fish & Mushroom Pie

Fish pie is a healthy and hearty dish for a hungry family. Mushrooms provide both flavor and texture.

Serves 4

INGREDIENTS
butter, for greasing
8 ounces assorted wild and cultivated
   mushrooms, trimmed and quartered
1½ pounds cod or haddock fillet,
   skinned and diced
2½ cups milk, boiling
salt and freshly ground black pepper

FOR THE TOPPING
2 pounds potatoes, quartered
2 tablespoons butter
⅔ cup milk
freshly grated nutmeg

FOR THE SAUCE
¼ cup unsalted butter
1 medium onion, chopped
½ celery stalk, chopped
½ cup all-purpose flour
2 teaspoons lemon juice
3 tablespoons chopped fresh parsley

1 Preheat the oven to 400°F. Butter an ovenproof dish, sprinkle in the mushrooms, add the fish and season with salt and pepper. Pour in the boiling milk, cover and cook in the oven for 20 minutes. Using a slotted spoon, transfer the fish and mushrooms to a 6¼-cup ovenproof dish. Pour the liquid into a pitcher and set aside.

2 Cover the potatoes with cold water, bring to a boil, add a pinch of salt and cook for 20 minutes. Drain and mash with the butter and milk. Season well with salt, pepper and nutmeg.

3 To make the sauce, melt the butter in a saucepan, add the onion and celery and sauté until soft, but not colored. Stir in the flour, then remove from heat.

4 Slowly add the reserved liquid, stirring well to combine. Return to the heat, stir and simmer to thicken. Add the lemon juice and parsley, season, then add to the dish.

FISH DISHES

5 Top the pie filling with the mashed potatoes and return to the oven for 30–40 minutes, until the topping is golden brown.

COOK'S TIP: This dish freezes well but should be completely defrosted before reheating.

Chicken Casserole with Blackberries & Lemon Balm

This delicious casserole combines some wonderful flavors, and the combination of red wine and blackberries gives it a dramatic appearance.

Serves 4

INGREDIENTS
4 chicken breasts, partly boned
2 tablespoons butter
1 tablespoon sunflower oil
¼ cup all-purpose flour
⅔ cup red wine
⅔ cup Chicken Stock
grated zest of ½ orange plus
    1 tablespoon juice
3 lemon balm sprigs, finely chopped,
    plus 1 sprig to garnish
⅔ cup heavy cream
1 egg yolk
⅔ cup fresh blackberries,
    plus ⅓ cup to garnish
salt and freshly ground black pepper

1 Remove any skin from the chicken, and season the meat. Heat the butter with the oil in a pan, fry the chicken to seal it, then transfer to a casserole.

2 Stir the flour into the pan, then add the red wine and the chicken stock and bring to a boil, stirring. Add the orange zest and juice and the chopped lemon balm. Pour the mixture onto the chicken in the casserole.

3 Preheat the oven to 350°F. Cover the casserole and bake for about 40 minutes.

4 Blend the cream with the egg yolk, add some of the liquid from the casserole and stir back into the dish with the blackberries (reserving those for the garnish).

5 Cover the casserole and cook for another 10–15 minutes. Serve immediately, garnished with the rest of the blackberries and a sprig of lemon balm.

Chicken, Leek & Parsley Pie

Flaky pastry with a creamy chicken filling makes a substantial and tasty supper for a cold winter's evening.

Serves 4–6

INGREDIENTS
2½ cups all-purpose flour
pinch of salt
scant 1 cup butter, diced
2 egg yolks

FOR THE FILLING
3 part-boned chicken breasts
flavoring ingredients (bouquet garni, black peppercorns, onion and carrot)
¼ cup butter
2 leeks, thinly sliced
½ cup grated Cheddar cheese
⅓ cup finely grated Parmesan cheese
3 tablespoons chopped fresh parsley
2 tablespoons whole-grain mustard
1¼ cups heavy cream
1 teaspoon cornstarch
salt and freshly ground black pepper
beaten egg, to glaze
mixed green salad, to serve

1 To make the pastry, sift the flour and salt. Blend together the butter and egg yolks in a food processor until creamy. Add the flour and process until the mixture is just coming together. Add 1 tablespoon cold water and process for a few seconds. Turn out onto a lightly floured surface and knead lightly. Wrap in plastic wrap and chill for about 1 hour.

2 Meanwhile, poach the chicken breasts in water to cover, with the flavoring ingredients, for about 30 minutes, until tender. Let cool in the liquid.

3 Preheat the oven to 400°F. Divide the pastry into two pieces. Roll out the larger piece on a lightly floured surface and use to line a 7 x 11-inch pie pan. Prick the crust with a fork and bake for 15 minutes. Let cool.

4 Lift the chicken from the poaching liquid and discard the skin and bones. Cut the flesh into strips, then set aside.

POULTRY, GAME & MEAT

5 Gently cook the leeks in the butter over low heat, stirring occasionally, until they are soft.

6 Stir in the cheeses and parsley. Spread half the leek mixture over the crust, leaving a border all the way around. Cover the leek mixture with the chicken strips, then top with the remaining leek mixture.

7 Combine the mustard, cream and cornstarch in a small bowl. Add seasoning to taste. Pour over the filling.

8 Moisten the edges of the crust. Roll out the remaining piece of pastry and use to cover the pie. Brush with beaten egg and bake for 30–40 minutes, until golden. Serve hot with a mixed green salad.

Roast Wild Duck with Juniper

There is little meat on the leg, so one duck will serve only two people—keep the legs for making a tasty stock.

Serves 2

INGREDIENTS
1 tablespoon juniper berries, fresh if possible
1 oven-ready wild duck
  (preferably a mallard)
2 tablespoons butter, softened
3 tablespoons gin
½ cup Chicken Stock
½ cup whipping cream
salt and freshly ground black pepper
watercress, to garnish

1 Preheat the oven to 450°F. Reserve a few juniper berries for garnishing and put the remainder in a heavy plastic bag. Crush coarsely with a rolling pin.

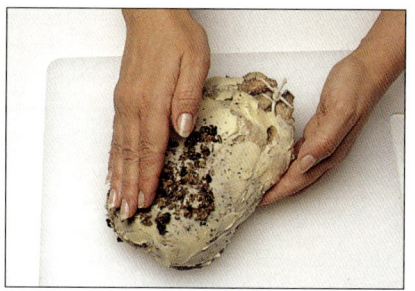

2 Wipe the duck with damp paper towels and remove any excess fat or skin. Tie the legs with string, then spread the butter over the duck. Sprinkle with salt and pepper and press the crushed juniper berries onto the skin.

3 Place the duck in a roasting pan and roast for 20–25 minutes, basting occasionally; the juices should run slightly pink when the thigh is pierced with a knife. Pour the juices from the cavity into the roasting pan and transfer the duck to a carving board. Cover loosely with aluminum foil and let stand for 10–15 minutes.

4 Skim off as much fat as possible from the roasting pan, leaving as much of the juniper as possible, and place the pan over medium heat. Add the gin and stir to combine, scraping the bottom of the pan, and bring to a boil.

5 Cook until the liquid has almost evaporated, then add the stock and boil to reduce by half. Add the cream and boil for 2 more minutes or until the sauce thickens slightly. Strain into a small saucepan and keep warm.

POULTRY, GAME & MEAT

6 Carve the legs from the duck and reserve for stock. Separate the thigh from the drumstick. Remove the breasts and arrange the duck in a warmed dish. Pour on a little sauce, sprinkle with the reserved juniper berries and garnish with watercress.

COOK'S TIP: Use the duck carcass as well as the legs to make a duck stock for other game dishes.

POULTRY, GAME & MEAT

Pheasant Breast with Apples

The tartness of apples perfectly complements the richness of pheasant in this wonderful traditional dish.

Serves 2

INGREDIENTS
2 boneless pheasant breasts
2 tablespoons butter
1 onion, thinly sliced
1 apple, peeled and quartered
2 teaspoons sugar
¼ cup Calvados
¼ cup Chicken Stock
¼ teaspoon dried thyme
¼ teaspoon white pepper
½ cup whipping cream
salt
sautéed potatoes, to serve

1 With a sharp knife, score the thick end of each pheasant breast.

2 In a heavy frying pan melt half the butter over medium heat. Add the onion and cook, stirring occasionally, for 8–10 minutes, until golden. Using a slotted spoon, transfer the onion to a plate.

3 Cut each apple quarter crosswise into thin slices. Melt half the remaining butter in the pan and add the apple slices. Sprinkle with the sugar and cook the apple slices over low heat, turning occasionally, for 5–7 minutes, until they are golden and caramelized. Transfer to the plate with the onion, then wipe out the pan.

4 Add the remaining butter to the pan and increase the heat to medium. Add the pheasant breasts, skin-side down, and cook for 3–4 minutes, until they are golden. Turn over and cook for another 1–2 minutes, until the juices run slightly pink when the thickest part of the meat is pierced with a knife. Transfer to a board and cover to keep warm.

COOK'S TIP: If you can't find Calvados, substitute Cognac, cider or apple juice instead.

POULTRY, GAME & MEAT

5 Add the Calvados to the pan and boil over high heat until reduced by half. Add the stock, thyme, a little salt and the pepper and reduce by half again. Stir in the cream, bring to a boil and cook for 1 minute. Add the sautéed onion and apple slices to the pan and cook for 1 more minute.

6 Slice each pheasant breast diagonally and arrange on warmed plates. Spoon on a little sauce with the onion and apples. Serve with the sautéed potatoes.

POULTRY, GAME & MEAT

Lamb Stew with Vegetables

Spring lamb and new vegetables make a mouthwatering combination.

Serves 6

INGREDIENTS
4 tablespoons vegetable oil
3 pounds lamb shoulder or other
   stewing meat, well trimmed,
   cut into 2-inch pieces
3–4 tablespoons all-purpose flour
4 cups Beef or Chicken Stock
1 large bouquet garni
3 garlic cloves, lightly crushed
3 ripe tomatoes, peeled, seeded and chopped
1 teaspoon tomato paste
1½ pounds small potatoes, peeled if desired
12 baby carrots, trimmed and scrubbed
4 ounces green beans, cut into 2-inch pieces
2 tablespoons butter
12–18 baby onions, peeled
6 medium turnips, peeled and quartered
2 tablespoons sugar
¼ teaspoons dried thyme
1½ cups peas
2 ounces snowpeas
3 tablespoons chopped fresh parsley
   or cilantro
salt and freshly ground black pepper

1 Heat 2 tablespoons of the oil in a frying pan over medium heat. Fry the lamb in batches, turning and adding more oil if needed. Transfer to a flameproof casserole when well browned. Add 3–4 tablespoons water and boil for 1 minute, scraping the bottom. Pour the liquid into the casserole.

2 Sprinkle the flour on the meat and set over medium heat. Cook for 3–5 minutes, until browned. Stir in the stock, bouquet garni, garlic, tomatoes, tomato paste and seasoning.

3 Bring to a boil over high heat, skimming off any foam. Reduce the heat and simmer, stirring occasionally, for about 1 hour, until the meat is tender. Cool the stew, then chill, covered, overnight.

4 Remove all the fat from the surface. Set the casserole over medium heat and bring to a simmer.

5 Cook the potatoes in salted water for 15–20 minutes, until tender, then, using a slotted spoon, transfer to a bowl and add the carrots to the same water. Cook for 4–5 minutes, until just tender and transfer to the bowl. Add the green beans and boil for 2–3 minutes, until tender. Transfer to the bowl.

POULTRY, GAME & MEAT

6 Melt the butter in a frying pan over medium heat. Add the onions and turnips with 3–4 tablespoons water and cook, covered, for 4–5 minutes. Uncover, stir in the sugar and thyme and cook, stirring occasionally, until the vegetables are caramelized. Transfer them to the bowl.

7 Add 2–3 tablespoons water to the pan and boil for 1 minute, scraping the bottom. Add to the lamb.

8 When the lamb and gravy are hot, add the vegetables and stir gently to distribute. Stir in the peas and snowpeas and cook for 5 minutes, until they turn bright green, then stir in 2 tablespoons of the parsley or cilantro and pour into a warmed serving dish. Sprinkle on the remaining parsley.

Lamb & Leeks with Mint

This is especially good with the new season's lamb and organic leeks.

Serves 6

INGREDIENTS
2 tablespoons sunflower oil
4½ pounds lamb (fillet or boned leg), cubed
10 scallions, thickly sliced
3 leeks, thickly sliced
1 tablespoon all-purpose flour
⅔ cup white wine
1¼ cups Chicken Stock
1 tablespoon tomato paste
1 tablespoon sugar
2 tablespoons finely chopped fresh mint, plus a few more leaves, to garnish
1 cup dried pears, chopped
2¼ pounds potatoes, peeled and sliced
2 tablespoons melted butter
salt and freshly ground black pepper

1 Heat the oil and fry the lamb to seal it. Transfer to a casserole. Preheat the oven to 350°F.

2 Cook the scallions and leeks for 1 minute, stir in the flour and cook for another minute. Add the wine and stock and bring to a boil. Add the tomato paste, sugar, salt and pepper with the mint and pears and pour into the casserole. Stir, then arrange the sliced potatoes on top and brush with the melted butter.

3 Cover and bake for 1½ hours. Then increase the temperature to 400°F and cook for another 30 minutes, uncovered, to brown. Garnish with mint leaves.

Bacon & Bean Stew

Serves 6

INGREDIENTS

¾ cup each dried black-eyed peas, pinto and cannellini beans, soaked overnight in cold water and drained
1 tablespoon olive oil
6 strips bacon
6 large country pork sausages
3 large carrots, halved
3 large onions, halved
1 small garlic bulb, separated into cloves
4 bay leaves
2 fresh thyme sprigs, plus extra to garnish
1–2 tablespoons dried green peppercorns
1¼ cups unsalted Vegetable Stock or water
1¼ cups red wine
salt and freshly ground black pepper

1 Boil a saucepan of water. Add the beans and boil vigorously for 30 minutes. Drain and set aside.

2 Pour the oil into a large, flameproof casserole, then lay the bacon on top. Add the sausages, carrots and onions. Peel the garlic cloves, then press them into the mixture with the herbs and peppercorns. Spoon the beans on top.

3 Pour in the stock or water and wine. Cover and bring to a boil. Reduce the heat and cook the stew for 4–6 hours, stirring periodically and adding liquid if necessary.

4 Stir the mixture and season to taste. Serve garnished with thyme.

Roast Pork with Sage, Marjoram & Celery Leaves

Pork is an inexpensive choice that is equally suitable for a family dinner or a celebratory meal. The fruit purée makes a delicious change from plain applesauce.

Serves 8

INGREDIENTS
6-pound cut of pork
3 tablespoons fresh sage
1 tablespoon fresh marjoram
3 tablespoons chopped celery leaves
¼ cup cider
salt and freshly ground black pepper

FOR THE PURÉE
2 apples
2 bananas
1 tablespoon butter
1 tablespoon Calvados

1 Preheat the oven to 325°F. Place the pork in the center of a large piece of aluminum foil. Mix the sage, marjoram and celery leaves together. Cover the fatty part of the pork with the herbs, season to taste and wrap tightly. Roast for about 1 hour.

2 Fold back the foil and baste the pork with the cider. Continue cooking, uncovered, for another hour, until a sharp knife pressed into the thickest part produces clear juices.

3 To make the purée, peel and slice the apples and bananas, put the butter in a pan and sauté the fruit.

4 Add the Calvados and set it on fire. When the flames have died down, remove the mixture from heat, put it in a food processor and purée. Serve the pork with the purée on the side.

COOK'S TIP: Suitable pork cuts for roasting include loin and leg.

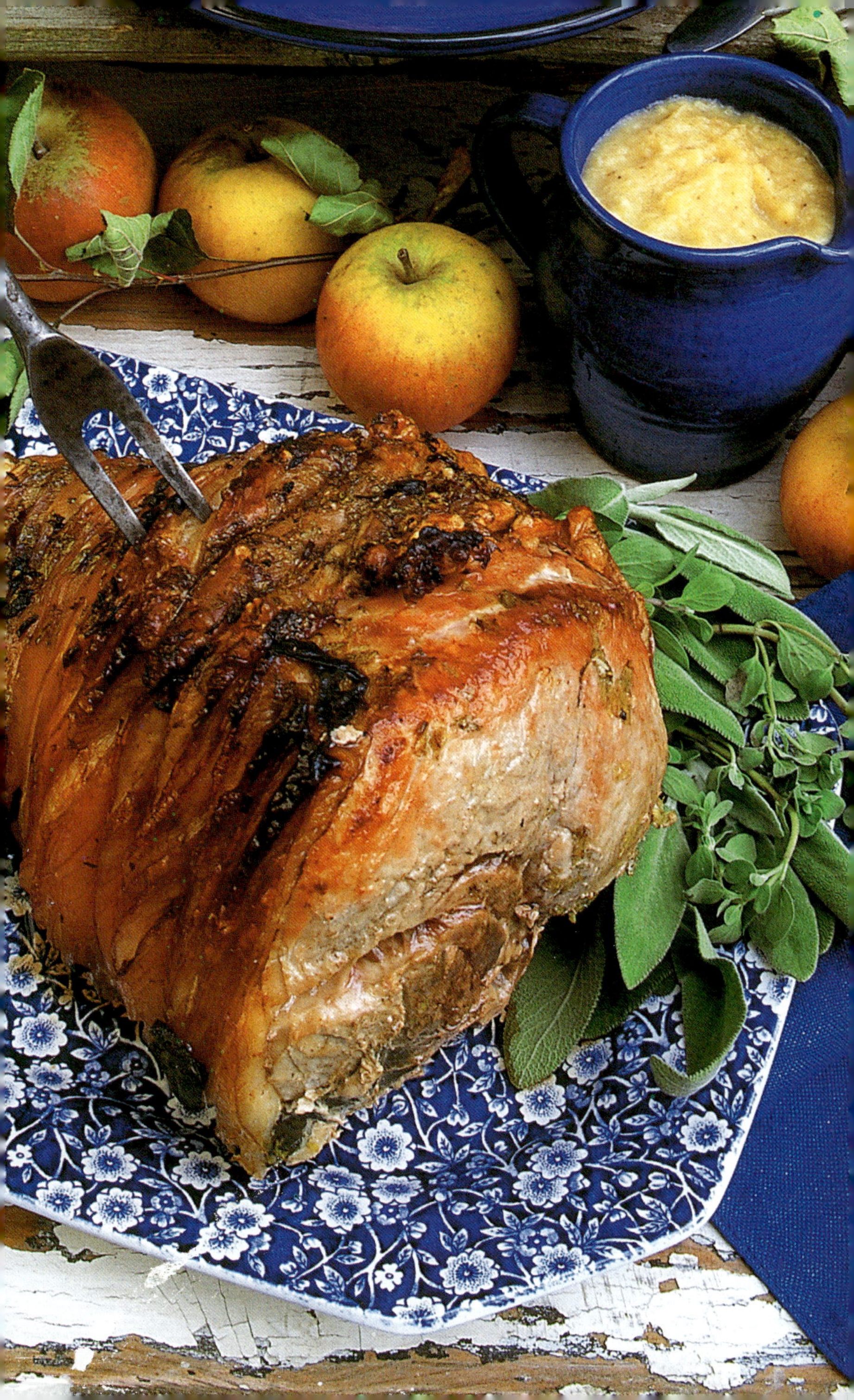

POULTRY, GAME & MEAT

Potroast with Beer

This heartwarming potroast is ideal for a winter's supper. Brisket has the best flavor, but this dish also works well with rolled topside.

Serves 6

INGREDIENTS
2 tablespoons oil
2 pounds rolled brisket of beef
10 ounces onions, roughly chopped
6 celery stalks, thickly sliced
1 pound carrots, cut into large chunks
1½ pounds potatoes, cut into large chunks
2 tablespoons all-purpose flour
2 cups Beef Stock
1¼ cups stout
1 bay leaf
3 tablespoons chopped fresh thyme, plus extra, to garnish
1 teaspoon brown sugar
2 tablespoons whole-grain mustard
1 tablespoon tomato paste
salt and freshly ground black pepper

1 Preheat the oven to 350°F. Heat the oil in a large flameproof casserole and brown the meat all over until it is golden. Remove from the pan and drain on paper towels.

2 Add the onions and cook, stirring constantly, for 4 minutes or until beginning to soften and turn brown.

3 Add the vegetables and cook over medium heat for 2–3 minutes, or until they are beginning to color.

4 Add the flour and cook for another minute. Blend in the stock and stout until combined. Bring to a boil, stirring.

5 Stir in the bay leaf, thyme, sugar, mustard, tomato paste and plenty of seasoning. Place the meat on top, cover tightly and transfer to the oven.

POULTRY, GAME & MEAT

6 Cook for about 2½ hours or until the vegetables and meat are tender. Adjust the seasoning and add another pinch of sugar, if necessary. Sprinkle with thyme leaves. To serve, remove the meat and carve into thick slices. Serve with the vegetables and plenty of beer gravy.

POULTRY, GAME & MEAT

Steak & Kidney Pie, with Mustard & Bay Leaf Gravy

This is a sharpened-up, bay-flavored version of a traditional favorite. The fragrant mustard, bay and parsley perfectly complement the rich, hearty flavor of the beef.

Serves 4

INGREDIENTS
1 pound puff pastry
3 tablespoons all-purpose flour
1½ pounds rump steak, cubed
6 ounces pig's or lamb's kidneys
2 tablespoons butter
1 medium onion, chopped
1 tablespoon mustard
2 bay leaves
1 tablespoon chopped parsley
⅔ cup Beef Stock
1 egg, beaten
salt and freshly ground
    black pepper

1 Roll out two-thirds of the pastry on a floured surface to about ⅛-inch thick. Line a 6¼-cup pie pan. Place a pie funnel in the middle.

2 Put the flour, salt and pepper in a bowl and toss the steak in the mixture. Trim and thickly slice the kidneys. Add to the steak and toss well. Melt the butter and sauté the onion until soft, then add the mustard, herbs and stock and stir well.

3 Preheat the oven to 375°F. Place the steak and kidneys in the pie and add the stock mixture. Roll out the remaining pastry to a thickness of ⅛ inch.

4 Brush the edges of the pastry forming the lower half of the pie with beaten egg and cover with the second piece of pastry. Press together to seal, then trim. Use the trimmings to decorate the top in a leaf pattern. Brush with beaten egg and make a small hole for the funnel. Bake for about 1 hour, until golden brown.

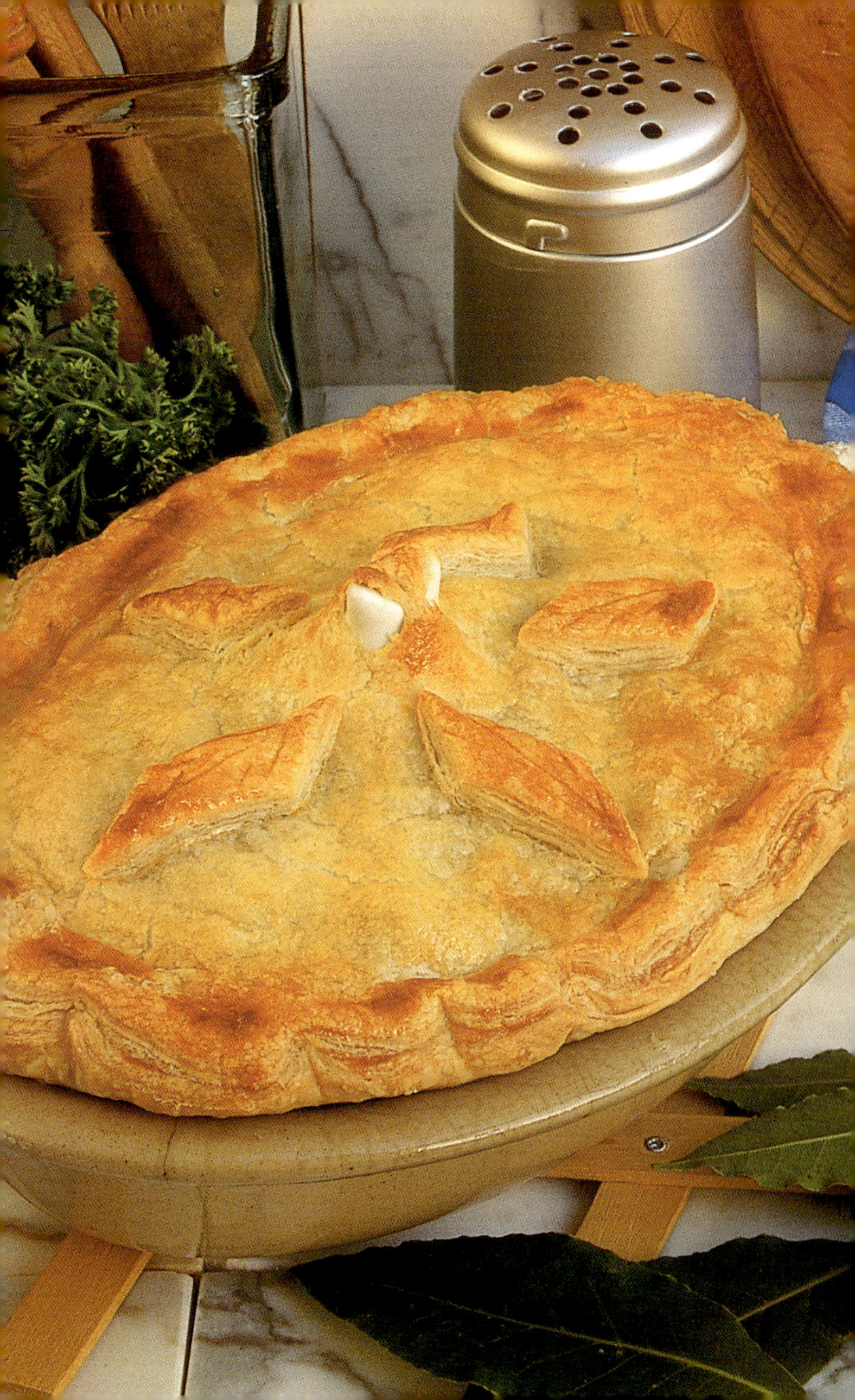

VEGETARIAN DISHES

Vegetable Casserole with Cheese Biscuits

Use a selection of your favorite vegetables for this wholesome dish.

Serves 6

INGREDIENTS
2 tablespoons oil
2 garlic cloves, crushed
1 onion, roughly chopped
1 teaspoon mild chili powder
1 pound potatoes, roughly chopped
1 pound celeriac, roughly chopped
12 ounces carrots, roughly chopped
12 ounces leeks, roughly chopped
3 cups mushrooms, halved
4 teaspoons all-purpose flour
2½ cups Vegetable Stock
14-ounce can chopped tomatoes
1 tablespoon tomato paste
2 tablespoons chopped fresh thyme
14-ounce can kidney beans,
   drained and rinsed
salt and freshly ground black pepper
fresh thyme sprigs, to garnish (optional)

FOR THE TOPPING
½ cup butter
2 cups self-rising flour
1 cup grated Cheddar cheese
2 tablespoons snipped fresh chives
about 5 tablespoons milk

1 Preheat the oven to 350°F. Heat the oil in a large flameproof casserole and sauté the garlic and onion for 5 minutes. Stir in the chili powder and cook for 1 minute.

2 Add the potatoes, celeriac, carrots, leeks and mushrooms. Cook for 3–4 minutes. Stir in the flour and cook for another minute.

3 Gradually stir in the stock with the tomatoes, tomato paste, thyme and seasoning. Bring to a boil, stirring. Cover and bake for 30 minutes.

4 Meanwhile, make the topping. Rub the butter into the flour, stir in half the cheese with the chives and seasoning. Add just enough milk to bind the mixture into a smooth dough.

VEGETARIAN DISHES

5 Roll out the dough until it is about 1 inch thick and cut into 12 triangles. Brush with a little milk.

COOK'S TIP: If you do use different vegetables, remember that you may need to adjust the cooking time according to their firmness.

6 Remove the casserole from the oven, add the beans and stir to combine. Place the triangles on top, overlapping slightly, and sprinkle with the remaining cheese. Return to the oven, uncovered, for 20–25 minutes or until golden brown and cooked through. Serve, garnished with fresh thyme sprigs, if using.

VEGETARIAN DISHES

Broccoli Crumble

Quick and easy to make this melt-in-your-mouth, creamy cheese-flavored broccoli dish has a crisp topping.

Serves 4

INGREDIENTS
2 tablespoons butter or margarine
2 leeks, thinly sliced
¼ cup all-purpose flour
⅔ cup milk
½ cup water
8 ounces broccoli, broken
   into florets
⅓ cup grated Parmesan cheese
salt and freshly ground black pepper

FOR THE TOPPING
1 cup all-purpose flour
1 teaspoon dried basil
6 tablespoons butter or margarine
1 cup fresh brown or
   white bread crumbs
pinch of salt

1 Preheat the oven to 375°F. Melt the butter or margarine in a flameproof casserole or saucepan and cook the sliced leeks for 2–3 minutes, until they are softened.

VARIATION: You might like to try using other vegetables in this tasty dish. Cauliflower makes a good substitute for the broccoli.

2 Stir in the flour and then gradually add the milk and water. Bring to a boil, add the broccoli and simmer, half-covered, over low heat for 5 minutes.

3 Stir in the Parmesan cheese, season with salt and pepper and pour into a medium-size ovenproof dish.

4 To make the topping, mix the flour with the basil and salt. Rub in the butter or margarine and then stir in the bread crumbs. Sprinkle on the broccoli and bake for 20–25 minutes, until the topping is golden brown.

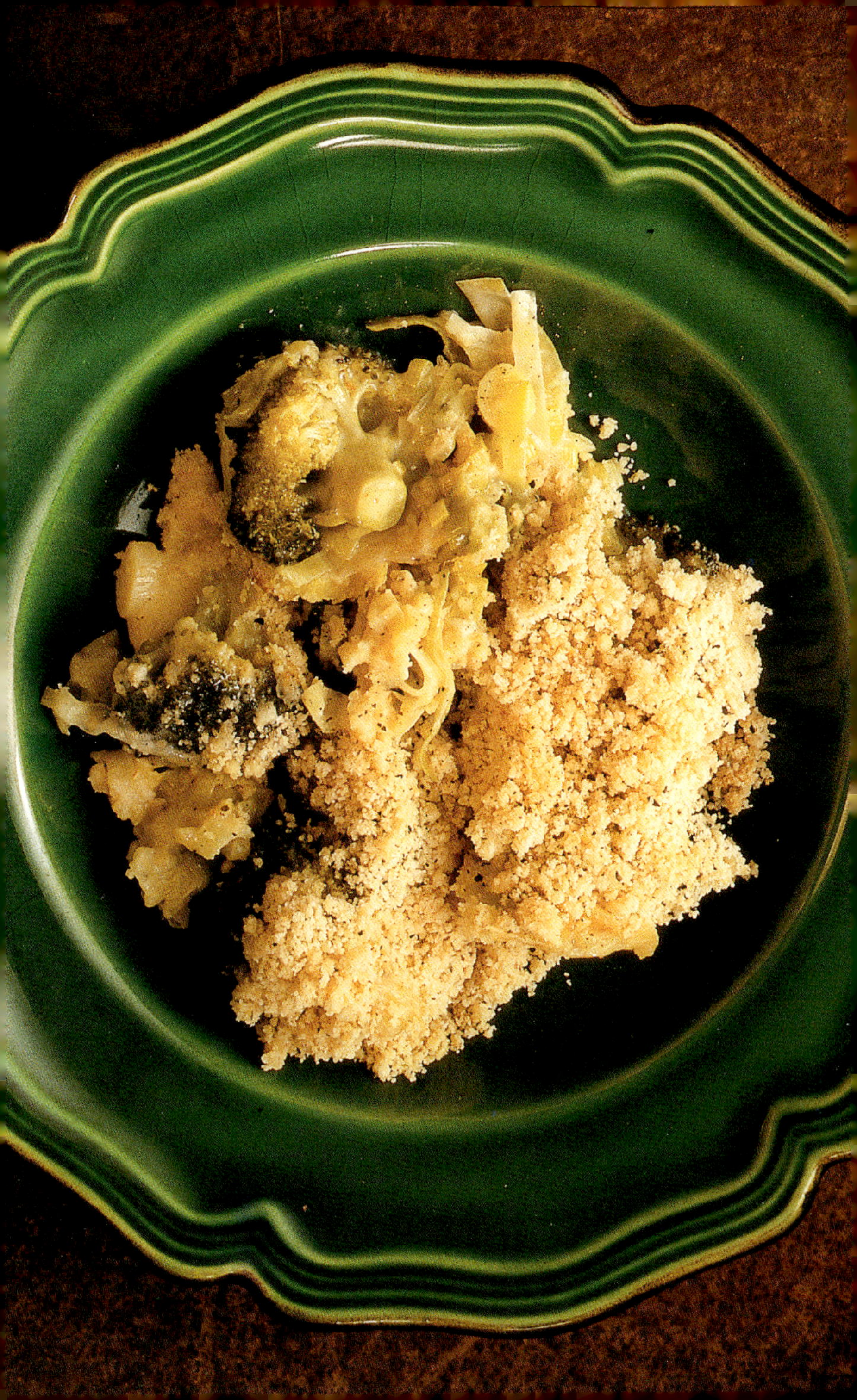

VEGETARIAN DISHES

Leek & Onion Tart

This unusual recipe isn't a normal tart with a pastry crust, but an all-in-one savory tart that has a rich flavor.

Serves 4

INGREDIENTS
¼ cup unsalted butter
12 ounces leeks, thinly sliced
8 ounces onion, chopped
2 cups self-rising flour
½ cup lard
⅔ cup water
salt and freshly ground
   black pepper

1 Preheat the oven to 400°F. Melt the butter in a heavy pan and sauté the leeks and onions until soft. Season to taste.

2 Off the heat, add the flour, lard and water to the leek mixture in the pan. Mix well to combine.

3 Place in a greased, shallow ovenproof dish that can be taken to the table, and bake for 30 minutes or until brown and crispy on the surface. Serve immediately in slices.

Creamy Layered Potatoes

Flavored with onions and baked in a rich, creamy sauce, these make a delicious change from roast potatoes.

Serves 6

INGREDIENTS
3–3½ pounds large potatoes, sliced
2 large onions, sliced
6 tablespoons unsalted butter
1¼ cups heavy cream
salt and freshly ground black pepper

the oven to 400°F. Blanch
tatoes for 2 minutes, and
ace the potatoes, onions,
ream in a large pan, stir
cook for about 15 minutes.

2 Transfer the potato and onion mixture to an attractive ovenproof dish. Season to taste with salt and freshly ground black pepper.

3 Bake for 1 hour, until the potatoes are tender, when pierced with the tip of a sharp knife, and lightly browned around the edges. Serve straight from the dish.

VEGETARIAN DISHES

Glazed Carrots with Cider

This recipe is extremely simple to make. The carrots are cooked in a minimum of liquid to bring out the best of their flavor, and the cider adds a pleasant sharpness.

Serves 4

INGREDIENTS
1 pound young carrots
2 tablespoons butter
1 tablespoon brown sugar
½ cup cider
¼ cup Vegetable Stock or water
1 teaspoon Dijon mustard
1 tablespoon finely chopped fresh parsley

1 Trim the tops and bottoms of the carrots. Peel or scrape them. Using a sharp knife, cut them carefully into julienne strips.

2 Melt the butter in a frying pan, add the carrots and sauté for 4–5 minutes, stirring frequently. Sprinkle on the sugar and cook, stirring, for 1 minute or until the sugar has melted.

3 Add the cider and stock or water, bring to a boil and stir in the Dijon mustard. Partially cover the pan and simmer for 10–12 minutes, until the carrots are just tender. Remove the lid and continue cooking until the liquid has reduced to a thick sauce.

VARIATION: For a change, try using finely chopped fresh rosemary instead of the parsley. This is an especially suitable variation for serving with roast lamb.

VEGETARIAN DISHES

4 Remove the pan from heat, and spoon into a warmed serving dish. Sprinkle the parsley on the carrots. Serve as an accompaniment to meat or fish or with a vegetarian dish.

COOK'S TIP: If the carrots are cooked before the liquid in the pan has reduced, transfer them to a serving dish and rapidly boil the liquid until thick. Pour onto the carrots and sprinkle with parsley.

Strawberry Fool

Make this delicious dessert on the day you want to eat it, and chill it well, for the best strawberry taste.

Serves 4

INGREDIENTS
1¼ cups milk
2 egg yolks
scant ½ cup sugar
few drops of vanilla extract
2 pounds ripe strawberries, plus 4 small strawberries, to decorate
juice of ½ lemon
1¼ cups heavy cream
4 sprigs of strawberry leaves or 4 fresh mint sprigs, to decorate

3 Gently heat and whisk until the mixture thickens (it should be thick enough to coat the back of a spoon). Lay a wet piece of waxed paper on top of the custard in the pan and let it cool.

1 First, make the custard by whisking 2 tablespoons milk with the egg yolks, 1 tablespoon sugar and the vanilla extract.

2 Heat the remaining milk until it is just below the boiling point. Stir the milk into the egg mixture. Rinse the pan out and return the mixture to it.

4 Purée the strawberries in a food processor or blender with the lemon juice and the remaining sugar until very smooth.

5 Lightly whip the cream and fold in the fruit purée and custard. Pour into glass dishes and decorate with the whole strawberries and strawberry leaves or mint sprigs.

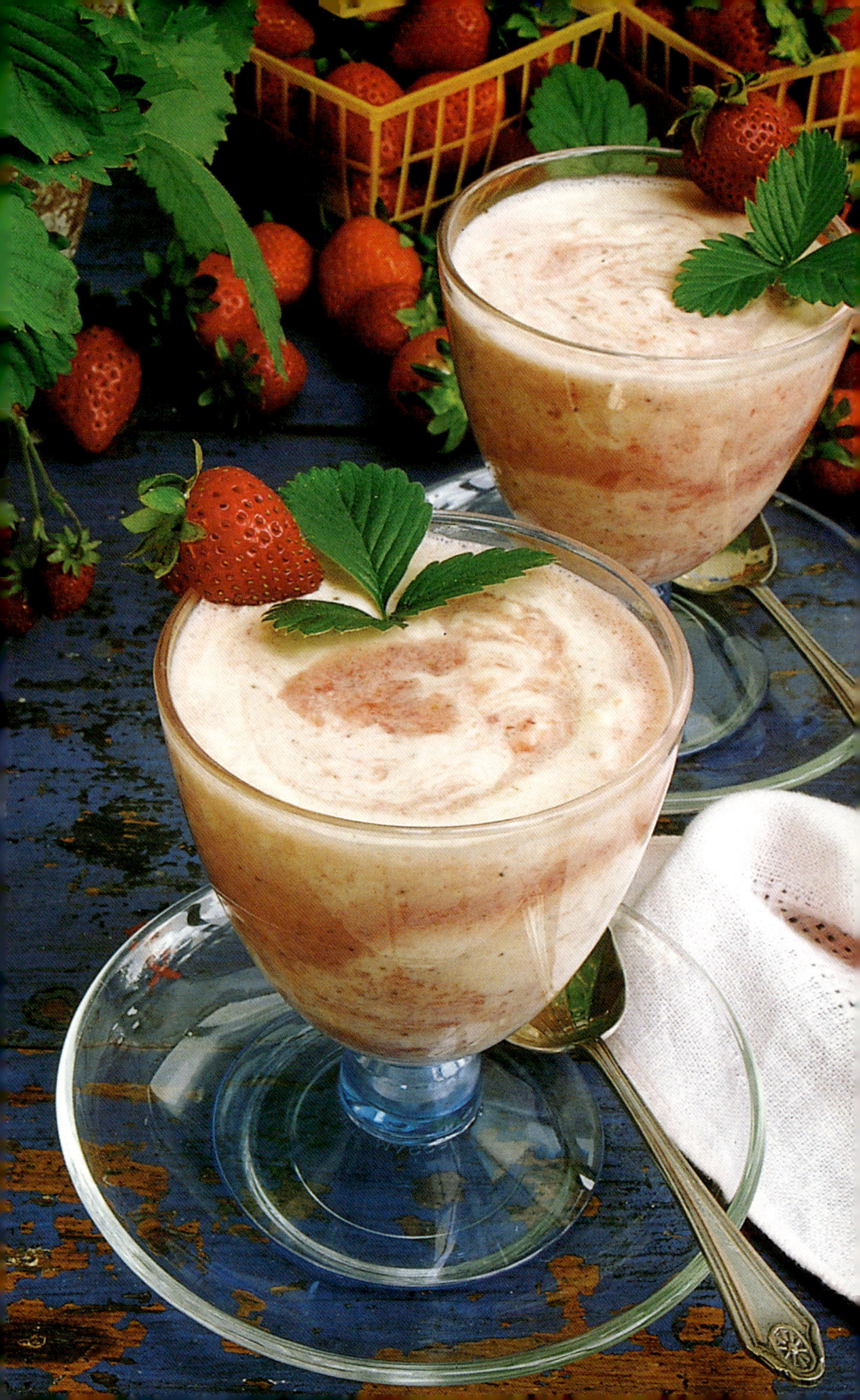

Bread Pudding with Currants

Fresh currants add a tart touch to this scrumptious dessert.

Serves 6

INGREDIENTS
8 medium-thick slices day-old bread, crusts removed
¼ cup butter, softened, plus extra for greasing
1 cup red currants
1 cup black currants
4 eggs, beaten
6 tablespoons sugar
2 cups milk
1 teaspoon pure vanilla extract
freshly grated nutmeg
2 tablespoons brown sugar
light cream, to serve

1 Preheat the oven to 325°F. Generously butter a 5-cup oval ovenproof dish.

2 Butter the bread generously, then halve diagonally. Layer in the dish, buttered-side up, sprinkling the currants between the layers.

3 Beat the eggs and sugar lightly together in a large mixing bowl, then gradually whisk in the milk, vanilla extract and a large pinch of freshly grated nutmeg.

4 Pour the milk mixture over the bread, pushing the slices down. Sprinkle the brown sugar and a little nutmeg on top. Place the dish in a roasting pan and fill with hot water to come halfway up the sides of the dish.

5 Bake for 40 minutes, then increase the temperature to 350°F and bake for 20–25 more minutes, or until the top is golden. Cool slightly, then serve with light cream.

VARIATION: This pudding is equally delicious made with other fresh fruits. A mixture of blueberries and raspberries would work just as well.

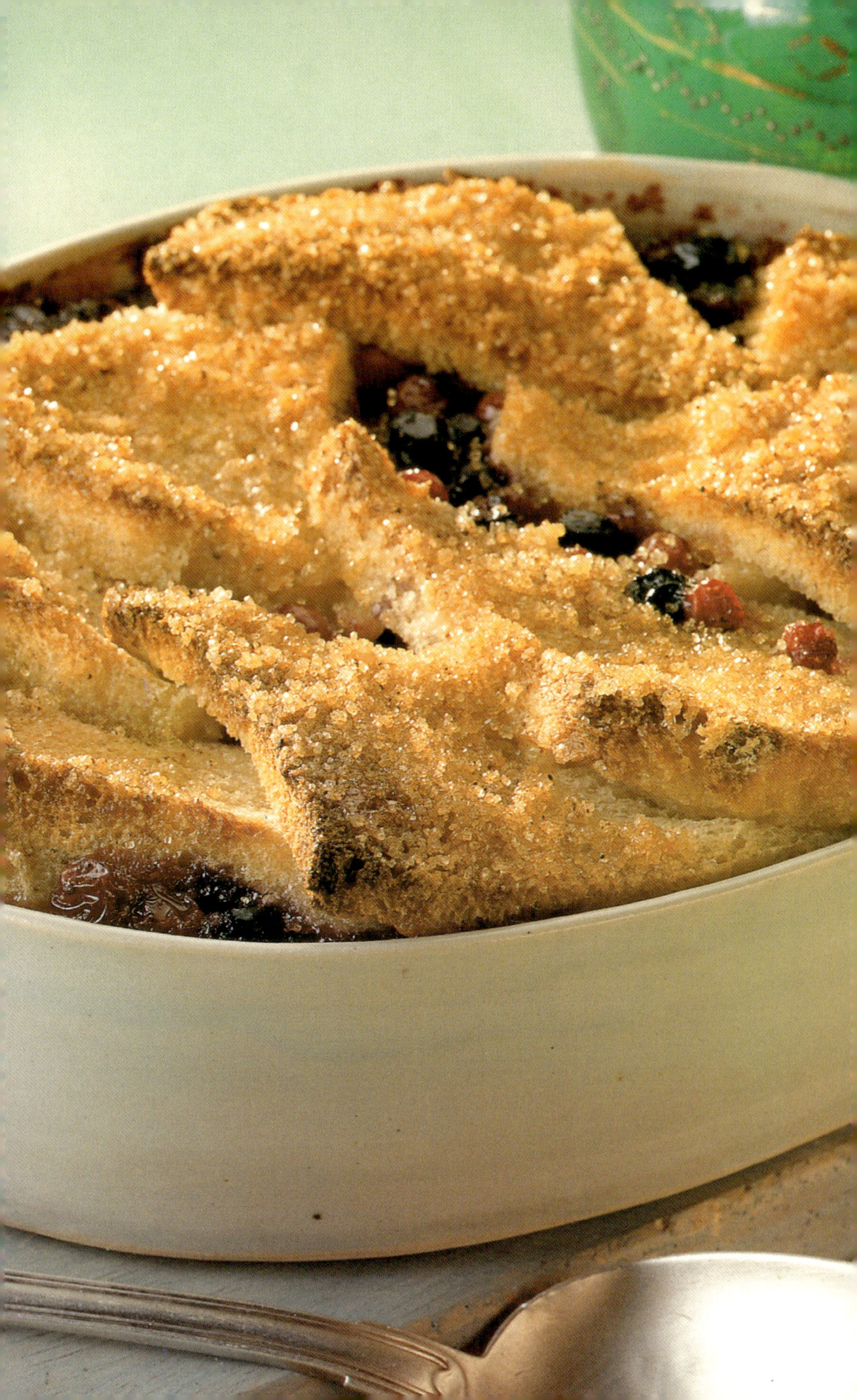

COUNTRY DESSERTS & BAKED GOODS

Spiced Apple Crumble

In this version of an ever-popular dessert, hazelnuts and cardamom seeds add a spicy crunchiness to the golden topping.

Serves 4–6

INGREDIENTS
butter, for greasing
1 pound apples
1 cup blackberries
grated zest and juice of 1 orange
¼ cup light brown sugar
custard, to serve

FOR THE TOPPING
1½ cups all-purpose flour
⅓ cup butter
⅓ cup sugar
¼ cup chopped hazelnuts
½ teaspoon crushed cardamom seeds

1 Preheat the oven to 400°F. Generously butter a 5-cup ovenproof dish. Peel and core the apples, then slice into the prepared dish. Level the surface, then sprinkle on the blackberries. Sprinkle the orange zest on top. Mix the orange juice and brown sugar and then pour over the fruit.

2 Set the fruit mixture aside while you make the topping. Sift the flour into a large bowl and rub in the butter until the mixture resembles coarse bread crumbs.

3 Stir in the sugar, hazelnuts and cardamom seeds. Sprinkle the topping on top of the fruit.

4 Press the topping around the edges of the dish to seal in the juices. Bake for 30–35 minutes or until the crumble is golden brown. Serve hot, with custard.

VARIATION: This crumble can be made with other types of fruit, as desired. Rhubarb with banana, pears, gooseberries and apricots would all be delicious.

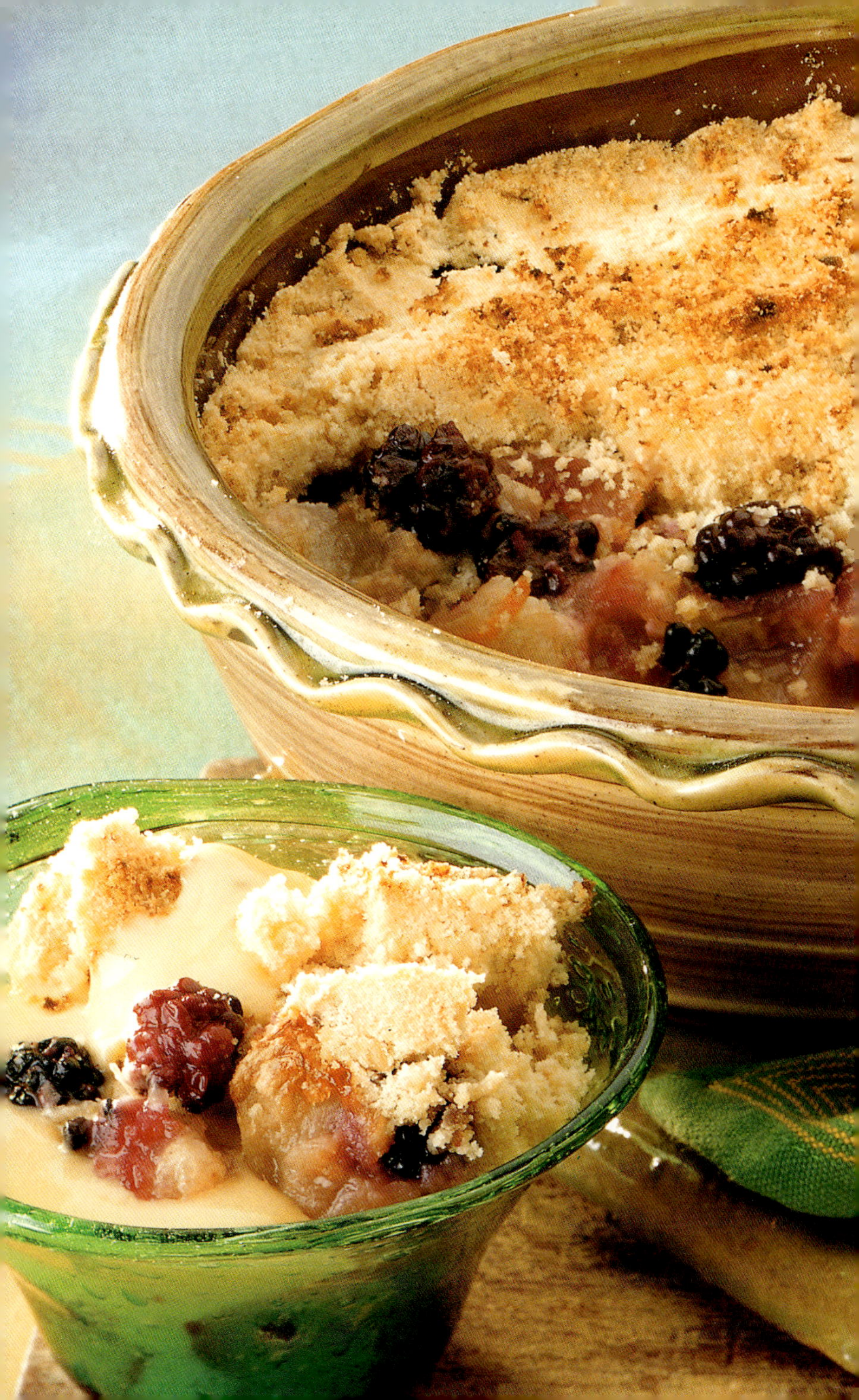

Pear & Blueberry Pie

This delicious, colorful pie, packed with autumn fruits and topped with crisp pastry, is totally irresistible.

Serves 4

INGREDIENTS
2 cups all-purpose flour
pinch of salt
¼ cup lard or vegetable shortening, cubed
¼ cup butter, cubed
6 cups blueberries
2 tablespoons sugar, plus additional, for sprinkling
1 tablespoon arrowroot
2 ripe, but firm pears, peeled, cored and sliced
½ teaspoon ground cinnamon
grated zest of ½ lemon
beaten egg, to glaze
crème fraîche, to serve

1 Sift the flour and salt into a bowl and rub in the lard or shortening and butter until the mixture resembles fine bread crumbs. Stir in 3 tablespoons cold water and mix into a dough. Chill for 30 minutes.

2 Place 2 cups of the blueberries in a pan with the sugar. Cover and cook gently for about 5 minutes, until the blueberries have softened. Press the mixture through a nylon sieve.

3 Blend the arrowroot with 2 tablespoons cold water and add to the blueberry purée. Bring to a boil, stirring until thickened. Cool slightly.

4 Place a baking sheet in the oven and preheat to 375°F. Roll out just over half the pastry on a lightly floured surface and use to line an 8-inch shallow pie pan.

5 Layer the remaining blueberries with the sliced pears on the pastry in the dish. Sprinkle with the ground cinnamon and lemon zest and pour the cooled blueberry purée on top.

COUNTRY DESSERTS & BAKED GOODS

6 Roll out the remaining pastry and use to cover the pie. Make a small slit in the center. Brush with egg and sprinkle with sugar. Bake the pie on the hot baking sheet for 40–45 minutes, until golden. Serve warm with crème fraîche.

Cheese Scones

These delicious scones make a good snack. They are best served fresh and still slightly warm.

Makes 12

INGREDIENTS
2 cups all-purpose flour
2½ teaspoons baking powder
½ teaspoon dry mustard powder
½ teaspoon salt
¼ cup butter, chilled
¾ cup grated Cheddar cheese
⅔ cup milk
1 egg, beaten

1 Preheat the oven to 450°F. Sift the flour, baking powder, mustard powder and salt into a mixing bowl. Add the butter and rub it into the flour mixture until the mixture resembles bread crumbs. Stir in ½ cup of the cheese.

2 Make a well in the center and add the milk and egg. Mix gently and then turn the dough out onto a lightly floured surface. Roll it out and cut it into triangles or squares.

3 Brush lightly with milk and sprinkle with the remaining cheese. Let rest for 15 minutes, then bake the scones for 15 minutes or until risen.

COUNTRY DESSERTS & BAKED GOODS

Dill & Potato Scones

Potato scones are quite delicious and should be made more often. Try this splendid combination, and you are sure to be converted.

Makes 10

INGREDIENTS
2 cups self-rising flour
3 tablespoons butter, softened
pinch of salt
1 tablespoon finely chopped fresh dill
scant 1 cup mashed potatoes, freshly made
2–3 tablespoons milk,
  as required

1 Preheat the oven to 450°F. Sift the flour into a bowl, and add the butter, salt and dill. Mix in the mashed potatoes and enough milk to make a soft, pliable dough.

2 Roll out the dough on a well-floured surface until it is fairly thin. Cut into neat rounds with a 3-inch cutter.

3 Bake the scones on a greased baking sheet for 20–25 minutes, until risen and golden.

This edition published by Southwater

Distributed in the UK by
The Manning Partnership, 251-253 London Road East, Batheaston, Bath BA1 7RL, UK
tel. (0044) 01225 852 727 fax. (0044) 01225 852 852

Distributed in the USA by
Ottenheimer Publishing, 5 Park Center Court, Suite 300, Owing Mills MD 21117-5001, USA
tel. (001) 410 902 9100 fax. (001) 410 902 7210

Distributed in Australia by
Sandstone Publishing, Unit 1, 360 Norton Street, Leichhardt, New South Wales 2040, Australia
tel. (0061) 2 9560 7888 fax. (0061) 2 9560 7488

Distributed in New Zealand by
Five Mile Press NZ, PO Box 33-1071, Takapuna, Auckland 9, New Zealand
tel. (0064) 9 4444 144 fax. (0064) 4444 518

All rights reserved. No part of this publication may be reproduced, stored in a retrieval system, or transmitted in any way or by any means, electronic, mechanical, photocopying, recording or otherwise, without the prior written permission of the copyright holder.

Southwater is an imprint of Anness Publishing Limited

© 2000 Anness Publishing Limited

A CIP catalogue record for this book is available from the British Library.

1 3 5 7 9 10 8 6 4 2

Printed and bound in Singapore

Publisher: Joanna Lorenz
Editor: Valerie Ferguson
Series Designer: Bobbie Colgate Stone
Designer: Andrew Heath
Editorial Reader: Penelope Gooodare
Production Controller: Joanna King

Recipes Contributed by: Carla Capalbo,
Carole Clements, Matthew Drennan,
Sarah Edmonds, Shirley Gill, Christine Ingram,
Maggie Mayhew, Katherine Richmond, Liz Trigg,
Steven Wheeler, Elizabeth Wolf-Cohen.

Photography: William Adams-Lingwood,
Karl Adamson, James Duncan, John Freeman,
Michelle Garrett, Amanda Heywood,
Patrick McLeavey, Thomas Odulate.